Poetry Writing and Study for N

Instructor Guide with activities, readings, and student quizzes

By Michelle Deerwester-Dalrymple

Introduction to the Course

The idea behind this course is to help instructors, teachers, charter schools, and home educators integrate creative writing into their middle school level courses.

This text is set up in a once a week format, allowing educators to integrate it into their current curriculum easily and, hopefully, seamlessly.

Poetry Writing and Study for Middle Grades is designed as an introductory writing text covering a board range of grades, with a specific focus on writing. Educators may want to include additional materials to focus more on different aspects of rhetoric and critical thinking for higher or more advanced students. Educators can also include the added activities, and separate grammar and language arts for a complete, semester long English credit class.

Throughout the semester, you can have students revise poems and resubmit them (highlighting the importance of the revision process!), create a final poetry portfolio of their favorite or best poems, or add art to a poem to create a visual poem. The work indicated by "in class" can be done with the parent or, if the student is able, on their own.

Michelle Deerwester-Dalrymple is a writer and a college writing professor. She has worked with students of all age levels – from elementary to graduate school – through her college teaching, tutoring, and charter school courses. She is currently working on other writing curricula texts and several novels. She lives in Southern California.

Also available:

Creative Writing for Junior and High School

Rhetoric: A Text for Middle and High School

Contents

Unit 1:

Vocabulary: adulation, adversity, circuitous

Writing Element – Acrostic Poem

An acrostic poem uses the letters of a word to form the beginning letter of each line of the poem. Even some of the Psalms from the Bible are acrostic in how they were written! Here is how an acrostic poem is structured: If you used the word "CAT," you would have a three-lined poem. The first line would begin with a "C." The second line would begin with an "A." The last line would begin with a "T." For example:

_____

CAT

Curious kittens

Always in trouble

Talks with a "meow"

_____

In class activity: Identify the Acrostic element in the poem below

*S*elect an animal (the name must be at least 5 letters long – butterflies, puppies, kittens, hamster, goldfish, raven, dolphin, seagull, etc . . .) Come up with a list of describing words/phrases for that animal. Use your five senses to really get a feel for your animal – the 5 senses are pivotal for writing poetry! Then, use the name of the animal (and your list of descriptions!) to write an acrostic poem describing it.

_____

*Reading: **Through the Looking Glass,** by Lewis Carroll from 1871*

A boat beneath a sunny sky,
Lingering onward dreamily
In an evening of July —
Children three that nestle near,
Eager eye and willing ear,

Pleased a simple tale to hear —
Long had paled that sunny sky:

Echoes fade and memories die.
Autumn frosts have slain July.
Still she haunts me, phantomwise,

Alice moving under skies
Never seen by waking eyes.
Children yet, the tale to hear,

Eager eye and willing ear,
Lovingly shall nestle near.
In a Wonderland they lie,
Dreaming as the days go by,

Dreaming as the summers die:
Ever drifting down the stream —
Lingering in the golden gleam —
Life, what is it but a dream?

Assignments:

1. Define and write Vocabulary words in sentences.

2. Follow the Acrostic model we worked on in class. **Write 2 more Acrostic poems**.

>   1: Use an element of nature (tree, stone, river, grass, sky, or another animal) to write an   acrostic poem describing it.

>   2. Select the name or the title of a person or character you have read about (in a book) and write an acrostic poem describing him/her.

Unit 2:

Vocabulary: collaborate, deleterious, aesthetic

Writing Element – Simile/ Metaphor

Simile is a comparison using the words "like" or "as"– for example "She is as clever as a fox" or "Your smile is like the sun." These are comparisons that use "like" or "as" and provide extra description. If you just write, "She has a bright smile," the reader may get the idea, but if you really want to convey just how brilliant that smile is, then use the comparison: "Her smile is as bright as the sun."

Metaphors do the same thing, but they don't use "like" or "as." You could write: "Love is a red rose" or "The diamond is a small piece of ice."

Read "the fog" by Carl Sandburg –

> The fog comes
>
> on little cat feet.
>
> it sits looking
>
> over harbor and city
>
> on silent haunches
>
> and then moves on.

Identify the simile/metaphor elements. Work on simile/metaphor poems.

_____

Class Worksheet:

Decide whether each sentence contains a simile or a metaphor

1. The baby was like an octopus, grabbing at all the cans on the grocery store shelves.

2. The giant's steps were thunder as he ran toward Jack.

3. The pillow was a cloud when I put my head upon it after a long day.

4. I feel like a limp dishrag.

5. Those girls are like two peas in a pod.

6. The fluorescent light was the sun during our test.

7. No one invites Harold to parties because he's a wet blanket.

8. The bar of soap was a slippery eel during the dog's bath.

Class activity- Metaphor/simile poem:

_____ is a _____ (something from nature)

It sounds like _____

It tastes as _____

It looks like _____

It smells like _____

(your topic) is _____

Reading: **Flint by** Christina Rossetti

An emerald is as green as grass,
A ruby red as blood;
A sapphire shines as blue as heaven;
A flint lies in the mud.

A diamond is a brilliant stone,
To catch the world's desire;
An opal holds a fiery spark;
But a flint holds a fire.

Assignments:

1. Define and write Vocabulary words in sentences.

2. Write 2 Metaphor/Simile poems at home, similar to what we did in class:

   1) You need to compare your topic to a color -- _____ is a _____ (pick a color)

   2) You need to compare your topic to an animal-- _____ is a _____ (an animal)

(Answers to Worksheet in Appendix 4)

Unit 3:

Vocabulary: superfluous, tenacious, venerable

Writing Element – Biography Poem

A Biography poem can be used to teach students to focus on the characteristics of a person or an animal, anything, or anyone really. It requires the students to put themselves in the subject's shoes. Share poems in class!

In Class Activity: Think of your sibling/friend/person

Line 1: Your character's first name

Line 2: Four words that describe your character

Line 3: Brother or sister of...

Line 4: Lover of...(three ideas or people)

Line 5: Who feels...(three ideas)

Line 6: Who needs...(three ideas)

Line 7: Who gives...(three ideas)

Line 8: Who fears...(three ideas)

Line 9: Who would like to see...

Line 10: Resident of

Line 11: His or her last name

Reading: A Character from a book:

Scout

Tomboy, brave, intelligent, loving

Sister of Jem

Lover of justice, chewing gum, reading, and Alabama summers

Who feels outrage when her dad is maligned, happiness when school is over, and fright on a dark Halloween night.

Who needs her dad's acceptance, Jem's loyalty, and Dill's admiration

Who gives friendship easily, black eyes to cousins, and sassy words to Calpurnia

Who fears Boo's dark house, owls in the night, and giving her open palms to the teacher

Who would like to see all mockingbirds sing freely whether they are creatures of flight, shy neighbors, or kind handymen

Resident of Maycomb, Alabama

Finch

Assignments:

1. Define and write Vocabulary words in sentences.

2. make a list of different adjectives/interests for bio poem.

3. **Write 2 Biography poems** at home, similar to what we did in class:

   1) Write about yourself;

   2) Write about pet or a character from a book or story.

Unit 4:

Vocabulary: vindicate, wary, resilient

Writing Element – AABB and ABAB

Poems can have different rhyming patterns to them. AABB means the first two lines rhyme, then the next to have a different rhyme:

Reading: **A Wise Old Owl by** Edward Hersey Richards

A wise old owl sat on an oak (A)

The more he saw the less he spoke; (A)

The less he spoke the more he heard; (B)

Why aren't we like that wise old bird? (B)

Some poems have a different structure, ABAB, in which every other line rhymes:

Reading: **An Apple Gathering**   by Christina Rossetti

I plucked pink blossoms from mine apple-tree (A)

   And wore them all that evening in my hair: (B)

Then in due season when I went to see (A)

   I found no apples there. (B)

Identify rhymes in poems presented. Are there any similes or metaphors? Select a picture for in class poem.

In Class Activity: Look at a picture or photograph of a nature scene. Come up with 2 rhyming pairs (4 words total) that describe it or your feelings about it. Write them into a poem that either rhymes AABB or ABAB. Share poems in class!

Assignments:

1. Define and write Vocabulary words in sentences

2. Write 2 poems at home similar to what we did in class, four lines each:

      1) a fun activity you like to do;

      2) a fruit or vegetable. Write one in AABB; write the other in ABAB.

Unit 5:

Vocabulary: Emulate; exemplary; longevity

Writing Element – Other Rhyming Schemes

Some poems have alternate rhyming schemes, like ABC or ABBA, or even ABCB. These schemes may combine with the ones we've already learned, or start their own, or change throughout the poem. Can you identify the rhyme scheme in the following poem? Give the same letter to the words that rhyme! (answer to activity in Appendix 4)

Reading except: **The Eagle** – By Alfred, Lord Tennyson

He clasps the crag with crooked hands:

Close to the sun in lonely lands,

Ringed with the azure world, he stands.

The wrinkled sea beneath him crawls;

He watches from his mountain walls,

And like a thunderbolt he falls.

-Identify rhymes in poems. Are there any similes or metaphors? What descriptive language is used? How does the poem make you feel? Work on Alternate rhymes.

In class activity: Think of your favorite toy or game. Come up with three rhyming words for it that describe it or your feelings about it. Write a 4-5 line poem using those three rhyming words, but not in AABB format. Share poems in class!

Assignments:

1. Define and write vocabulary words in sentences.

2. Write 2 poems at home similar to what we did in class, four lines each:

1) an animal;

2) a friend or sibling.

Don't use ABAB or AABB!

Unit 6:

Vocabulary: sagacity, censure, amicable

Writing Element – Idiom

An idiom is a common phrase or saying that most people are familiar with:

- Catch forty winks (get a quick nap) ,
- Count your blessings (be thankful for what you have),
- Every cloud has a silver lining (bad things usually have a good side to them), The grass it always greener on the other side (that someone else has something better, no matter what it is),
- Great oaks from little acorns grow (that even the smallest seed can grow into something mighty),
- A penny saved is a penny earned (if you save your money instead of spend it , it's almost like earning money),
- steal your thunder (when someone does something extraordinary before you),
- Where there's a will, there's a way (if you want something badly enough, you fill find a way to get it).

Reading excerpt: **Mending Wall -- by Robert Frost**

Something there is that doesn't love a wall,

That wants it down." I could say "Elves" to him,

But it's not elves exactly, and I'd rather

He said it for himself. I see him there

Bringing a stone grasped firmly by the top

In each hand, like an old-stone savage armed.

He moves in darkness as it seems to me,

Not of woods only and the shade of trees.

He will not go behind his father's saying,

And he likes having thought of it so well

He says again, "Good fences make good neighbours."

Think of other idioms. Identify rhymes in poems. Are there any similes or metaphors? What descriptive language is used? How does the poem make you feel? Work on idiom poem in class *In Class Activity:* Can we think of some more famous sayings? Then, select one idiom and then note some ideas, feelings or symbols you find in that idiom. Then write a four line poem about it. Share poems in class!

Assignments:

1. Define and write vocabulary words in sentences.

2. Write 2 Idiom poems at home based on two idioms that you select. You can choose from our list or think of one on your own. If you aren't sure you know any, you can look up "Idioms" on the internet. Use whatever rhyming scheme you have learned so far.

Unit 7:

Vocabulary: anecdote, disdain, mundane

Writing Element – Haiku

Haiku is beautiful, delicate poetry develop hundreds of years ago in Japan. Haiku is usually about an aspect of nature: plants, earth, water, animals, the sky. The poem has two thoughts in it. The first part is an observation about nature. The second is the poet's feelings or emotions about it. Each Haiku has a standard format:

Line 1 – 5 syllables

Line 2 – 7 syllables

Line 3 - 5 syllables

Remember, syllables are phonetic separation within a word: o/pen for open; ro/bot; for robot; at/ti/tude for attitude. Haiku does not have to say every part or idea; you can suggest things to the reader or leave it up to their imagination. Also remember that Haiku does not have to rhyme!

Reading: Hyakuichi

Thinking comfortable

Thoughts with a friend in silence

In the cool evening.

Basho

An old silent pond . . .

Into the pond a frog jumps,

Splash! Silence again.

Identify rhymes in poems. Are there any similes or metaphors? What descriptive language is used? How does the poem make you feel? Work on haiku poem in class.

In Class Activity: You are going to write haiku about a flower. Pick any type of flower. Be sure to think of your flower using all 5 senses, to help you write your Haiku. Then think of how your observations make you feel. Put that all together to write a Haiku. Share poems in class!

Assignments:

1. Define and write vocabulary words in sentences.

2. Write 2 haiku at home. The first one should be about either earth or water, the second should be about an animal.

Vocabulary Quiz! No vocab – vocab test!!!

Writing Element – Couplet

A couplet can be found in any rhyming scheme and occurs when two lines of a stanza or poem have their own rhyme. The Poem can read AABB, the AA is a couplet, and BB is a couplet. The poem can be ABAB but then end with CC; the CC is the couplet. Shakespeare's Poetry is famous for its couplets at the end! Can you identify the couplets in Frost's poem below?

_____

The Road not Taken --Robert Frost

Two roads diverged in a yellow wood,
And sorry I could not travel both
And be one traveler, long I stood
And looked down one as far as I could
To where it bent in the undergrowth;
Then took the other, as just as fair,
And having perhaps the better claim,
Because it was grassy and wanted wear;
Though as for that the passing there

Had worn them really about the same,
And both that morning equally lay
In leaves no step had trodden black.
Oh, I kept the first for another day!
Yet knowing how way leads on to way,
I doubted if I should ever come back.
I shall be telling this with a sigh
Somewhere ages and ages hence:
Two roads diverged in a wood, and I-
I took the one less traveled by,
And that has made all the difference.

_____

Identify rhymes in poems. Are there any similes or metaphors? An idiom? What descriptive language is used? How does the poem make you feel? Work on poem in class.

In Class Activity: Think of a recent event or activity you participated in. Jot down some ideas, feeling, and descriptions of that event. Write a 6 line poem with any rhyme scheme, but the last two lines much end in a couplet. Share poems in class!

Assignments:

Write 2 Couplet poems at home.

1. The first one should be about either a friend or family member

2. The second should be about a famous location or travel spot you have been to recently (e.g. the Grand Canyon, a light house, a bridge, a river, the zoo, a windmill, a campground, whatever you can think of!)

For each poem, write a 6 line poem with any rhyme scheme, but the last two lines much end in a couplet. (answer in Appendix 4)

Unit 9:

Vocabulary: asylum, benevolent, camaraderie

Writing Element – Alliteration

Repeating the same initial consonant sound in neighboring words: "Tiny Tommy Tucker traded tables with Tammy Turner on Tuesday." Using alliteration can make a big impact on your poem, or it can make the poem sound more musical. Or it can really emphasize something. Can you identify the alliterative elements below? (answers in Appendix 4)

Reading: *I see the boys of summer* - Dylan Thomas 1914-1953

I see the boys of summer in their ruin

Lay the gold tithings barren,

Setting no store by harvest, freeze the soils;

There in their heat the winter floods

Of frozen loves they fetch their girls,

And drown the cargoed apples in their tides.

Identify rhyme scheme. Are there any similes or metaphors? Any idioms? Any couplets? What descriptive language is used? How does the poem make you feel? Find the alliteration.

In Class Activity: Think of several lists of words that all begin with the same letter or sound. Use your vocabulary lists to help you! Use those lists to write a short 4-line poem! Share poems in class!

Assignments:

1. Define and Write Vocabulary words in sentences.

2. Write 2 Alliterative poems at home. You pick the length and format!

      1. The first should be on a sport that you like to watch or play.

      2. The second should be on one of your favorite places.

Be sure to try and include elements you have been learning in class like metaphors, similes, haiku, and couplet!

Unit 10:

Vocabulary: fortuitous, frugal, abhor

Writing Element – Japanese Lantern Poem

Japanese Lantern Poems use alliteration to create feeling and a picture in the reader's mind of whatever subject the writer chose. A lantern is a light and airy Japanese poem that follows a syllabic pattern as follows:

Line 1: one syllable (noun)
Line 2: two syllables (describing noun)
Line 3: three syllables (describing noun)
Line 4: four syllables (describing noun)
Line 5: one syllable (another word for the noun in line one)

Reading:

Leaves
burning
blowing down

gold, red, and brown
Fall

Sky
so blue
many clouds
above the earth
now

Work on Lantern Poems—look at samples: Are there any similes or metaphors? Any idioms? Any couplets? What descriptive language is used? How does the poem make you feel? Find the alliteration.

In Class Activity: Think of your favorite story or scene. Pick one element from that scene and think of several words and ideas that describe it or describe how it makes you feel. Try to use words that start with the same letter or sound, as we did with the alliterative poems. Use as many of those words as possible to create an alliterative lantern poem. Write a Lantern poem following the format. Share poems in class.

Assignments:

1. Define and write Vocabulary words in sentences.

2. Write 2 Lantern poems at home.

    1.   Poem #1 – a person you admire (family member or friend)

    2.   Poem #2: an element of nature.

Follow the models from class – remember to use as much alliteration as you can!

Vocabulary: Faint; opulent; prudent

Writing Element – Cinquain

This is a type of poem based on haiku – called cinquain. These poems only have 5 lines (in French, the work for 5 is *cinq)*. Cinquain does not have to have an end rhyme. Here is the typical patter for cinquain:

Line 1: Title ………………………2 syllables

Line 2: describes Title …………….4 syllables

Line 3: expresses action…………..6 syllables

Line 4: expresses feeling…………..8 syllables

Line 5: another work for the Title…2 syllables

Reading: *November Night* **by Adelaide Crapsey 1878-1915**

Listen . . .

With faint dry sound

Like steps of passing giants

The leaves, frost crisp'd, break from the trees

And fall.

Identify rhyme scheme. Are there any similes or metaphors? Any idioms? Any couplets? Alliteration? What descriptive language is used? How does the poem make you feel? Bring a picture and have the students write in class poem based on the picture.

In Class Activity: Look at the picture in class – Come up with words and feelings that you get from the picture write one cinquain about the picture, using the format.

Assignments:

1. Define and write Vocabulary words in sentences.

2. Write 2 cinquain poems at home.

　　1. For the first one, find either a photo or a picture you really like and write about it.

　　2. For the second one, select one of the four seasons, and write about that.

Vocabulary: florid, quarrel, rancor

Writing Element – Onomatopoeia

Onomatopoeia are words that sound like the objects they name or the sounds those objects make. " Zip" is an onomatopoeia word because it sounds like a jacket is zipping up. Identify the onomatopoeia in the poem below. (answer in Appendix 4)

Reading: **THE BELLS -** by Edgar Allan Poe (1849)
Hear the sledges with the bells-
Silver bells!
What a world of merriment their melody foretells!
How they tinkle, tinkle, tinkle,
In the icy air of night!

Identify rhyme scheme. Are there any similes or metaphors? Any idioms? Any couplets? Alliteration? Identify the Onomatopoeia. What descriptive language is used? How does the poem make you feel? Sport or activity poem in class.

In Class Activity: Think of your favorite sport or activity. What sounds do you hear with it? Write down all (or at least 4) the sounds you hear, what made the sound, then compare it to something else that makes a similar sound. Put all those line together to make on poem. Share poems in class.

Assignments:

1. Define and write Vocabulary words in sentences.

2. Write 2 poems at home.

> 1. Poem #1 - Listen to the sounds you hear in nature – a river, animals, the wind . . . Pick one of those elements to write about. Write down all (or at least 4) the sounds that element would make, then compare it to something else that makes a similar sound. Put all those line together to make on poem.

> 2. Poem #2: Listen to the sounds in your house on an average day. Write down the different sounds you hear, what makes those sounds, and how those sounds make you feel (happy, excited, warm and fuzzy, smiley . . .)

Vocabulary: Nuance, Renown, Tangent

Writing Element – Free Verse – bring a picture to class meeting

FREE VERSE is a kind of poetry that has no real rhythm or pattern, so you can put words together in all sorts of ways. You can be VERY imaginative! In free verse the writer makes his/her own rules. The writer decides how the poem should look, feel, and sound. Henry David Thoreau, a great philosopher, explained it this way, ". . . perhaps it is because he hears a different drummer. Let him step to the music which he hears, however measured or far away." It may take you a while to "hear your own drummer," but free verse can be a great way to express what you really feel.

Reading: "This is Just to Say" by William Carlos Williams

I have eaten

the plums

that were in

the icebox

and which

you were probably

saving

for breakfast

forgive me

they were delicious

so sweet

and so cold

Free Verse. Explain what it is. Look at poem. Are there any similes or metaphors? Any idioms? Any couplets? Alliteration? Onomatopoeia? What descriptive language is used? How does the poem make you feel?

In Class Activity: Look at your picture in class. Make some notes in class that describes the picture, but also include other descriptions that you know of that may not be present in the picture. Also write down some ideas and feelings you have about this picture or the person in it. Combine those ideas into a free verse poem. Remember you don't have to rhyme! Just share your emotions and descriptions about your topic!

—

Assignments:

1. Define and write Vocabulary words in sentences.

2. Write 2 Free Verse poems at home.

> 1. Poem #1 - Think of your favorite food – make some notes, using your 5 senses to describe the food. Also add to the list your feelings about that food. Then combine those into your own free verse poem.

> 2. Poem #2: Think of your favorite toy. Again, make some notes, using your 5 senses to describe the toy. Also add to the list your feelings about that toy. Then combine those into your own free verse poem.

Remember you don't have to rhyme with these poems! Just share your emotions and descriptions about your topic!

Unit 14:

Vocabulary: Billowing, Cower, Hamper

Writing Element – Shape Poem/Concrete Poem

Shape or concrete poems are descriptive poems that are written in the shape of the topic of the poem. The poem can either be in the shape of the topic (example #1) or the poem can be written as the outline of the topic shape (example #2).

Reading: In a Twist; The Altar -George Herbert

In a twist

We felt the rain, wind, and hail, and
Then the thunder and lightning came.
The winds gathered up and began to spin
Like a spinning top, sucking up dust like a vacuum cleaner.
The twister went around and around, like a merry-go-round.
The gusts of air were picking up dust.
It continued to roar loudly,
Destroying everything
Along the way.
Soon it was
Gone.

ken A L T A R, Lord, thy servant reares,
of a heart, and cemented with teares:
Whose parts are as thy hand did frame;
No workmans tool hath touch'd the same.
A H E A R T alone,
Is such a stone,
As nothing but
Thy pow'r doth cut.
Wherefore each part
Of my hard heart
Meets in this frame,
To praise thy Name:
That, if I chance to hold my peace,
These stones to praise thee may not cease,
t thy blessed S A C R I F I C E be mine,
sanctifie this A L T A R to be thine.

Identify rhyme scheme or is it free verse? Are there any similes or metaphors? Any idioms? Any couplets? Alliteration? Onomatopoeia? What descriptive language is used? How does the poem make you feel? .

In Class Activity: Think of an item you can pick up (a ball, a fruit, a snack, a toy, a leaf, a flower, etc …) and come up with a list of words that describe it. Use at least one metaphor or simile, and one onomatopoeia that will help describe your item. Do a quick sketch of the item on your paper, then either write the poem to fill up that shape, or write it around the edge of that shape to create your shape poem. Share with class.

Assignments:

1. Define and write Vocabulary words in sentences.

2. Write 2 shape poems at home.

1. Poem #1 – Pick a basic shape (square, triangle, circle). Select an item that is similar to that shape. Following the model in class, write a shape poem about that item in the shape you selected.

2. Poem #2: Take an item from nature with a basic shape, and write a shape poem about it in the shape of that item. Follow the format we used in class!

Vocabulary: Enhance, Labyrinth, Kindle

Writing Element – Appreciating poetry!

There are many famous poems and poets throughout time. It is a good idea to recognize "great" poetry or classical poetry to help broaden your understanding of poetry and writing overall. You can also you "great" poetry as a model to help you write poetry as well. Try to apply some of the elements we have learned over the semester to this poem.

Reading: "The Tyger" William Blake (first stanza)

Tyger! Tyger! burning bright,
In the forests of the night,
What immortal hand or eye
Could frame thy fearful symmetry?

In what furnace was thy brain?

What the anvil? what dread grasp,

Dare its deadly terrors clasp!

In what distant deeps or skies.

Burnt the fire of thine eyes?

On what wings dare he aspire?

What the hand, dare seize the fire?

And what shoulder, & what art,

Could twist the sinews of thy heart?

And when thy heart began to beat,

What dread hand? & what dread feet?

What the hammer? what the chain,

Identify rhyme scheme or is it free verse? Are there any similes or metaphors? Any idioms? Any couplets? Alliteration? Onomatopoeia? What descriptive language is used? How does the poem make you feel?

In Class Activity: For this assignment, think of an animal. Write down the animal and some descriptions of it. Try to think of a comparison, metaphor, or simile for it as well. Then come up with a question or two you have for that animal – any question at all.

To write the poem, write the animal name two times, then follow with the description of your animal. These will be the first two lines. The second two lines need to be your question. If you can make the lines rhyme, or create couplets, please do! BUT don't force it if you can't make it rhyme!

Assignments:

1. Define and write Vocabulary words in sentences.

2. Write 2 Blake-style poems at home.

> 1. Poem #1 - Follow the format from class. Select another animal and write a Blake style poem.
>
> 2. Poem #2: Again, follow the format from class. Think of another item from nature and write about Blake-style poem about it.

Work on revising any of your poems that you think need more work and come to class next week, ready to share some of your poems in class! Select at least 3 to share!

Unit 16:

Final Vocabulary quiz!

Share poems in class! Analyze yours or another student's poems: Identify rhyme scheme or is it free verse? Are there any similes or metaphors? Any idioms? Any couplets? Alliteration? Onomatopoeia? What descriptive language is used? Why did the student select those elements? How does the poem make you feel?

APPENDIX 1: VOCABULARY DEFINITIONS

<u>Unit 1</u>

Adulation: high praise

Adversity: misfortune

Circuitous: indirect, roundabout

<u>Unit 2</u>

Collaborate: to work together

Deleterious: harmful; having a negative effect

Aesthetic: pertaining to the arts or beauty

<u>Unit 3</u>

Superfluous: more than enough; extraneous, extra or more than necessary

Tenacious: persistent, resolute

Venerable: respectable due to age; to hold sacred

<u>Unit 4</u>

Vindicate: to clear from blame; to free

Wary: watchful, alert

Resilient: quick to recover; able to become refreshed

<u>Unit 5</u>

Emulate: follow by example; to mimic another

Exemplary: outstanding; the best example

Longevity: long life

Unit 6

Sagacity: to verify, confirm, truthful

Censure: to criticize harshly

Amicable: friendly, agreeable

Unit 7

Anecdote: a story or a short account of events

Disdain: to regard with scorn or distaste

Mundane: ordinary, common, boring; unoriginal

Unit 8

No vocabulary – Vocabulary mid term! (Appendix 2)

Unit 9

Asylum: sanctuary, safe place

Benevolent: kind, caring or helpful

Camaraderie: trust among friends

Unit 10

Fortuitous: lucky, happening by chance

Frugal: thrifty, spendthrift

Abhor: deep hate

Unit 11

Faint: soft, light, not loud

opulent: wealthy, well decorated

prudent: careful, cautious

Unit 12

Florid: ornate; decorative

Quarrel: to fight or argue

Rancor: deep-seated ill will or resentment

Unit 13

Nuance; something subtle, a fine shade of meaning

Renown: fame

Tangent: going off the main subject

Unit 14

Billowing: swelling, fluttering, waving

Cower: recoil in fear or servility, shrink away

Hamper: hinder; obstruct

Unit 15

Enhance: improve, make better or clearer

Labyrinth: a maze/puzzle

Kindle: to start a fire

Unit 16

No vocabulary. Final Vocabulary Exam (Appendix 3)

Vocabulary Quiz 1   **Name**_____

                              Total points: _____/15

Match the word with the correct definition by writing the matching letter for the definition on the line.

Matching Set 1:

_____1. adulation   a. persistent, resolute

_____2. adversity   b. to regard with scorn or distaste

_____3. circuitous   c. high praise

_____4. tenacious   d. indirect, roundabout

_____5. venerable   e. misfortune

_____6. resilient   f. ordinary, common

_____7. disdain   g. respectable due to age

_____8. mundane   h. quick to recover

Matching Set 2:

_____1. Superfluous   a. a story or a short account of events

_____2. Emulate: b. long life

_____3. exemplary   c. to criticize harshly

_____4. longevity   d. extra/more than enough

_____5. censure   e. friendly, agreeable

_____6. amicable   f. outstanding

_____7. anecdote   g. follow by example

Vocabulary Quiz 1

\text{Name}_____\text{KEY}_____

Total points: _____/15

Match the word with the correct definition by writing the matching letter for the definition on the line.

Matching Set 1:

_c___1. adulation   a. persistent, resolute

_e___2. adversity   b. to regard with scorn or distaste

_d___3. circuitous   c. high praise

_a___4. tenacious   d. indirect, roundabout

__g__5. venerable   e. misfortune

_h___6. resilient   f. ordinary, common

__b__7. disdain   g. respectable due to age

_f___8. mundane   h. quick to recover

Matching Set 2:

__d__1. Superfluous   a. a story or a short account of events

_g___2. Emulate: b. long life

_f___3. exemplary   c. to criticize harshly

_b___4. longevity   d. extra/more than enough

c____5. censure   e. friendly, agreeable

__e__6. amicable   f. outstanding

_a___7. anecdote   g. follow by example

Vocabulary Quiz 2   **Name**_____

                                         Total points: _____ /15

Match the word with the correct definition by writing the matching letter for the definition on the line.

Matching Set 1:

_____1. sanctuary   a. cautious

_____2. benevolent   b. fame

_____3. Faint   c. something subtle

_____4. opulent   d. kind, caring

_____5. prudent   e. safe place

_____6. Nuance   f. soft, not loud

_____7. Renown   g. wealthy

Matching Set 2:

_____1. camaraderie   a. going off the main subject

_____2, Tangent   b. thrifty

_____3. fortuitous   c. ornate; decorative

_____4. frugal   d. trust among friends

_____5. Abhor   e. fluttering; waving

_____6. florid   f. deep-seated resentment

_____7. rancor   g. hate

_____8. Billowing   h. lucky

Name__KEY_____

                                         Total points: _____/15

Match the word with the correct definition by writing the matching letter for the definition on the line.

Matching Set 1:

_e___1. sanctuary   a. cautious

__d__2. benevolent   b. fame

__f__3. Faint   c. something subtle

_g___4. opulent   d. kind, caring

_a___5. prudent   e. safe place

_c___6. Nuance   f. soft, not loud

__b__7. Renown   g. wealthy

Matching Set 2:

__d__1. camaraderie   a. going off the main subject

_a__2, Tangent   b. thrifty

h____3. fortuitous   c. ornate; decorative

_b___4. frugal   d. trust among friends

__g__5. Abhor   e. fluttering; waving

c____6. florid   f. deep-seated resentment

_g___7. rancor   g. hate

_e___8. Billowing   h. lucky

APPENDIX 4: Answers to Unit Activities

Unit 2: *In Class Activity:*

S   1. The baby was like an octopus, grabbing at all the cans on the grocery store shelves.

M   2. The giant's steps were thunder as he ran toward Jack.

M   3. The pillow was a cloud when I put my head upon it after a long day.

S   4. I feel like a limp dishrag.

S   5. Those girls are like two peas in a pod.

M   6. The fluorescent light was the sun during our test.

M   7. No one invites Harold to parties because he's a wet blanket.

M   8. The bar of soap was a slippery eel during the dog's bath.

Unit 5: In class activity:

Reading except: **The Eagle** – By Alfred, Lord Tennyson

He clasps the crag with crooked hands: (A)

Close to the sun in lonely lands,   (A)

Ringed with the azure world, he stands. (A)

The wrinkled sea beneath him crawls; (B)

He watches from his mountain walls, (B)

And like a thunderbolt he falls.   (B)

Unit 8: In Class Activity

And be one traveler, long I stood (COUPLET)

And looked down one as far as I could (COUPLET)

Two roads diverged in a wood, and I— (COUPLET)

I took the one less traveled by, (COUPLET)

Unit 9: IN class Activity-

I see the boys of summer in their ruin

Lay the gold tithings barren,

Setting no store by harvest, freeze the soils;

There in their heat the winter floods

Of frozen loves they fetch their girls,

And drown the cargoed apples in their tides.

S – "summer" "setting" "soils"

F – "freeze" "floods" "frozen" "fetch"

Unit 12: in class activity

tinkle, tinkle, tinkle, - onomatopoeia

Appendix 5: Extra Activities

If your students need extra activities, are more advanced critical thinkers, or you want to make this more of a full semester English credit, the follow is a list of activities you can assign to compliment the material in this text

1. For each unit, have the students apply the concepts to a poem they locate either online or in a book, identifying the different poetic elements.

2. For the same poem, have the students identify the concepts and how well the students feel the concepts were implemented, in 1-2 paragraph papers.

3. As students advance in their lessons, have them go back to previous unit poem readings and apply the newer concepts for more dynamic learning.

4. Integrate an interdisciplinary approach and have students apply the concepts learned to other classes, such as reading of classical literature, or poems from other cultures or English-speaking countries.

5. Once students are comfortable completing a poetic analysis, have the students write papers comparing two or more poems on the devices used, how well those elements were implemented, and which poem the student feels was more successful or creative in the presentation of those poetic elements.

Made in the USA
Las Vegas, NV
07 June 2021